FRESH START

Welcome to your new life!

ALSO BY JOEL OSTEEN

Break Out!

Break Out! Journal

Daily Readings from Break Out!

I Declare

I Declare Personal Application Guide

Every Day a Friday

Every Day a Friday Journal

Daily Readings from Every Day a Friday

You Can, You Will

You Can, You Will Journal

Your Best Life Now

Daily Readings from Your Best Life Now

Starting Your Best Life Now

Your Best Life Now Study Guide

Your Best Life Now for Moms

Your Best Life Begins Each Morning

Your Best Life Now Journal

FRESH START

Welcome to your new life!

JOEL OSTEEN

Unless otherwise indicated, all Scripture quotations are taken from the *New King James Version* of the Bible. Copyright © 1982 by Thomas Nelson, Inc. Used by permission. All rights reserved.

Scripture quotations noted NLT are taken from the *Holy Bible*, New Living Translation, copyright © 1996, 2004, 2007 by Tyndale House Foundation. Used by permission of Tyndale House Publishers, Inc., Carol Stream, Illinois 60188. All rights reserved.

Scripture quotations noted AMP are from *The Amplified Bible*. Copyright © 1954, 1958, 1962, 1964, 1965, 1987 by The Lockman Foundation. All rights reserved. Used by permission. (www.Lockman.org)

Scripture quotations noted KJV are from the *King James Version* of the Holy Bible.

Scripture quotations noted NIV are taken from *The Holy Bible, New International Version*® NIV®. Copyright © 1973, 1978, 1984, 2011 by Biblica, Inc.™ Used by permission. All rights reserved worldwide.

All Scriptures marked NASB are from the *New American Standard Bible*®, Copyright © 1960, 1962, 1963, 1968, 1971, 1972, 1973, 1975, 1977, 1995 by The Lockman Foundation. Used by permission.

Literary development and interior design: Koechel Peterson & Associates, Inc., Minneapolis, Minnesota

Joel Osteen Ministries
1-888-567-JOEL
1-800-278-0520
(Customer Service)
PO Box 4600
Houston, TX 77210

Printed in the United States of America

ISBN: 978-1-4555-91534

Acknowledgments

My first thanks, as always, goes to God for guiding me through the writing process. Next up, among those I'm grateful for are my friends at Hachette Book Group for their help. Also, I am thankful for the creative insight from our Lakewood Church pastoral staff member Steve Austin.

I am grateful also to my literary agents, Shannon Marven and Jan Miller Rich, at Dupree Miller & Associates, who are once again proved invaluable throughout the entire process. Special thanks go to wordsmith Wes Smith, who is always there when I call.

Once again, this book includes many stories shared with me by friends, members of our congregation, and people I've met around the world. I appreciate and acknowledge their contributions and support. Some of those mentioned in the book are people I have not met personally, and, in a few cases, we've changed the names to protect the privacy of individuals. I give honor to all of those to whom honor is due.

As the son of a church leader and a pastor myself, I've listened to countless sermons and presentations, so in some cases I can't remember the exact source of a story. Thanks to all who have touched my life with theirs. My intention in writing this book is to pass on the blessings, and to God be the glory.

Contents

Introduction 9

Chapter 1 15
The Goodness of God

Chapter 2 23
God Is a Rewarder

Chapter 3 31
The Power of Letting Go

Chapter 4 39
Thinking Yourself to Victory

Chapter 5 47
The Power of Your Vision

Chapter 6 55
The Power of "I Am"

Chapter 7 63
Being Selective about What You Feed Yourself

Chapter 8 71
Deal with It

Appendix 1 79
Scriptures on Managing Our Thought Life

Appendix 2 83
Scriptures on the Power of Our Words

Appendix 3 87
Daily Positive Confessions

Prayer of Salvation 91

Next Steps 93

INTRODUCTION

He shall be like a tree

Planted by the rivers of water,

That brings forth its fruit in its season,

Whose leaf also shall not wither;

And whatever he does shall prosper.

PSALM 1:3

Introduction

Congratulations on making the best decision of your life—to live your life with God at the center. Scripture talks about how life with God is like a tree and its branches. When a branch is connected to the tree, it receives nourishment and life. It's able to produce fruit. In the same way, we have to stay connected to God so we can receive His strength and be empowered to accomplish all that He has for us.

In any relationship, growth happens over time. God doesn't expect you to be perfect. He doesn't expect you to know everything. He just wants you to keep moving forward with Him one step at a time. He wants to show you His goodness and be a part of your everyday life. It may feel a little strange at first, but just like any new relationship, the more time you spend with Him, the more comfortable it becomes. That's why I wrote this book—to help you connect with God and learn about His ways!

Today, know that God is bigger than your past, your disappointments, and your problems. You may have made a lot of mistakes, but God can turn those things around. People may have hurt you, but if you'll trust God, He'll restore you. Just stay focused on the new life you have with Him. Think of it like a change in seasons. When winter turns to spring, the old is gone and the new begins. The past may have been cold and dreary. Maybe your dreams have been dormant and covered. But now it's Springtime! Spring symbolizes a fresh start. It's a time for new growth and multiplication!

You may not see all the changes you want right away, but remember, you don't see the fullness of spring instantly either. It takes time for the leaves to grow back and the blossoms unfold. It doesn't happen all at once, and neither do things with God. Just trust that He is at work bringing about good in every area of your life.

As you read these pages, be open to what God will reveal to your heart. No matter what's going on in your day-to-day life, keep making time for Him so that your relationship can grow strong and you can walk in the fullness of the blessing He has prepared for you!

Maybe your dreams have been dormant and covered. But now it's Springtime! Spring symbolizes a fresh start. It's a time for new growth and multiplication!

The
GOODNESS
of GOD

Every good gift and every perfect gift is from above, and comes down from the Father of lights.

JAMES 1:17

CHAPTER 1

The Goodness of God

Just like the sun radiates heat, God radiates goodness. It's not just what He does; it's who He is. God's very nature is good. It's important that we recognize God's goodness. The Scripture says *every* good gift comes from our Father in Heaven, both large and small.

Too many times, God is working in our lives, showing us favor, protecting us, sending us healing, but we don't recognize His goodness. Don't take things for granted. It wasn't a coincidence that you met your spouse and fell in love. God was directing your steps. It wasn't a lucky break that you got that job. It was God's hand of favor. The fact that your children are strong and healthy is not just good fortune. That's God being good to you. All through the day we should be saying, "Thank You, Lord, for Your goodness. Thank You for my health. Thank You for my spouse. Thank You for the opportunities and good breaks You've given me."

You need to be on the lookout for God's goodness. Our attitude should be, "I can't wait to see what God is going to do today." Anything good that happens, be quick to give God the credit. It may be something small. Maybe you suddenly have a good idea. "Lord, thank You for that idea. I know it came from You." You finish a project at work sooner and easier than you expected. "Lord, thank You for Your grace with that project." God is constantly working, showing us His goodness, but too many times we don't recognize it. We're waiting for the big, spectacular things.

The Scripture says every good gift comes from our Father in Heaven, both large and small.

Whenever something good happens, I'm going to give God thanks. When I see favor, "Thank You, Lord." When I'm reminded of something I need to do, "Thank You, Lord." When somebody lets me in on the freeway, "Thank You, Lord." When the temperature drops below 100 in Houston, "Thank You, Lord." When I'm protected, "Thank You, Lord." When I see the breakthrough, "Thank You, Lord." I'm talking about living with an attitude of thankfulness and gratefulness. God blesses a thankful attitude.

When something good happens, you're seeing God. Make sure you thank Him for it. Make sure you give Him the credit. You may not think God is doing anything in your life, but God is constantly showing us His goodness. My question is: Are you recognizing it? Look around this week. Be more aware. Psalm 34:8 says, "Oh, taste and see that the LORD is good." If you're going to taste God's goodness, you have to realize that every good break, every time you were protected, every door that opened, and every advantage you've gotten has been God working in your life. Don't take it for granted.

I heard about this man who was driving around a crowded parking lot trying to get a space, going around and around. He got so frustrated that he finally said, "God, if You'll give me a parking spot, I'll go to church every Sunday." Right then, immediately, a car backed out of a space, and as he pulled in, he said, "Never mind, God. I just found one." That's the way we are a lot of times. We forget that every good thing comes from God.

Every one of us can look back and remember times God protected us, spared us from an accident, gave us a promotion, caused us to be at the right place at the right time, or made a way when there seemed to be no way. Don't ever get tired of thanking God for His goodness. Remember your victories. Tell the people around you. Keep bragging

> *If you're going to taste God's goodness, you have to realize that every good break, every time you were protected, every door that opened, and every advantage you've gotten has been God working in your life.*

on the goodness of God. The more you brag on God's goodness, the more of God's goodness you'll see.

Too many times today instead of remembering our victories we're remembering our defeats, our failures, our disappointments. When we remember what God has done for us, it causes faith to rise in our hearts. We know if God did it for us before, He can certainly do it for us again.

I encourage you to do three things:

1. *Expect* God's goodness. Get up every day looking for God's favor.
2. *Recognize* God's goodness. There are no coincidences, no lucky breaks. It's the goodness of God.
3. Always *thank* God for His goodness. Whenever something good happens, large or small, be quick to thank God for it. Live with an attitude of gratitude and praise.

If you do these things, you'll experience more of God's goodness and favor, and your life will go to a whole new level.

Action Plan

But be doers of the word,
and not hearers only . . .
JAMES 1:22

1. Get into the habit of thanking God throughout the day for every blessing, big and small.

2. Start a "Blessing Journal" and write down every significant blessing, breakthrough, or promotion God brings your way. When you're tempted to get discouraged, look through the journal and remind yourself of everything God has done in your life.

3. Psalm 9:11 tells us to declare God's good works among the people. Tell others about the good things God does in your life and give Him credit. It will encourage them and strengthen their faith and give glory to God.

GOD IS
a
REWARDER

[God] is a rewarder of those who diligently seek Him.

HEBREWS 11:6

CHAPTER 2

God Is a Rewarder

The greatest key to living a life filled with God's blessings and favor is to keep God first place in your life. When you put God first place and make it your highest priority to please Him, you can expect to live a blessed, fulfilled life. Hebrews 11:6 states, "God is a rewarder of those who diligently seek Him." Notice who God rewards. Not people who half-heartedly seek Him, only seek Him when they have a problem, or come to church only on special occasions. God rewards people who *diligently* seek Him. Psalm 34:10 adds: "Those who seek the LORD shall not lack any good thing." When you seek God daily with your whole heart, you won't be able to outrun the good things of God.

What's interesting about a reward is that it is put in place before anyone claims it. Right now, there are rewards for certain fugitives who are on the loose. The money is already in a fund waiting for someone to step up and claim it. All they have to do is find the fugitive and the money will be released in that fund. In the same way, God has a reward that has already been put in place. It's just waiting to be released. The only catch is we have to meet the demands of the reward. God makes it so easy: "You don't even have to find Me. If you will just *seek* Me—if you will get up in the morning and thank Me, read My Word, and make an effort to please Me—I will give you the reward."

Jesus said in Matthew 6:33, "Seek *first* the kingdom of God and His righteousness, and all these things shall be added to you." Notice the key: seek *first* the Kingdom. In other words, don't seek the blessing; seek the Blessor. Don't be consumed by things. Don't chase after money, fame, fortune, bigger this, bigger that. Chase after God. If you will seek the Blessor, He promises all these other things will be added unto you. Not a few things; *all* these things. God is a God of abundance. When you keep Him first place, you won't be able to contain all the good things He will bring across your path. Instead of chasing blessings, blessings will chase you.

Sometimes we get up in the morning and think, "I don't want to read my Bible today. I don't feel like going to church. I'm tired." But once you develop the habit and see the benefit of how you feel refreshed and restored, make better decisions, and have God's favor, you'll think, "I can't afford *not* to do this." You'll realize that spending time with God is vital to living a victorious life.

The last few months of my father's life he was on dialysis. Three times a week for four hours a day he would go to the clinic to have his blood cleansed. There were times he didn't feel like going. He was tired or busy or wanted to do something else. It didn't matter; he went anyway. Why? His life depended on it. It wasn't an option. It was vital. My father loved to travel all over the world, but when he started dialysis, he had to change his plans and rearrange his priorities. He knew how important dialysis was to him.

Don't be consumed by things. Don't chase after money, fame, fortune, bigger this, bigger that. Chase after God.

That's the way we need to see seeking God. Require it as a vital necessity. When things get busy, the children need you, it's hectic at the office, you've got a thousand things to do, you've got to put your foot down and say, "No, this is not an option. If I'm going to be strong, if I'm going to be my best today, if I'm going to have God's favor, I've got to rearrange my priorities so I can spend time with God."

You may have to get up earlier—before the children need you, before checking your emails, before the phone starts ringing. Take time to invest in your spiritual well-being. We feed our physical body at least three meals a day, but often we feed our spirit just once a week at church. We wonder why we feel burned out, unenthusiastic, and lack favor, wisdom, and creativity. It's because we're not taking time to get filled back up. Just like we feed our physical man, we need to feed our spiritual man. When you invest in your spiritual well-being, it will pay huge dividends in your life.

In God's presence there is fullness of joy, fullness of peace, fullness of victory.

The Scripture says that in God's presence there is fullness of joy, fullness of peace, fullness of victory. That's where you're refreshed and restored. Take time at the beginning of each day to sit quietly in His presence, pray, and read your Bible. These days, life can be so busy, hectic, and noisy. But when you get alone with God and put Him first, the rest of your day will go much better. All through the day, meditate on God's promises. Put on some good praise music. If you diligently seek Him, you will reap rich rewards and live the abundant life He has for you.

Action Plan

But be doers of the word,
and not hearers only . . .
JAMES 1:22

1. Try to spend at least the first 30 minutes with God every morning, reading His Word, praying, putting Him first before work or other priorities.
2. Acknowledge God throughout the day, thanking Him for your blessings and seeking His guidance and wisdom.
3. Develop a habit of stopping to pray and seek God's will before making any important decision.

The POWER
of
LETTING
GO

Forgetting those things

which are behind . . .

I press toward . . .

<small>PHILIPPIANS 3:13–14</small>

CHAPTER 3

The Power of Letting Go

We all go through disappointments, setbacks, and trials we don't understand. Maybe you prayed for a loved one, but they didn't get well. You stood in faith for a relationship, but it didn't work out. You did your best in your job or business, but things didn't go like you planned. One of the best things you can do is release it. Let it go.

We can't walk in victory and receive all that God has in our future if we don't learn to release negative experiences. When we hold on to those experiences, dwelling on negative thoughts and emotions, wondering why it didn't work out, it opens the door to bitterness, resentment, and self-pity. We

We can't walk in victory and receive all that God has in our future if we don't learn to release negative experiences.

start blaming others, ourselves, or even God. We may not understand it. It may not have been fair. But when we give it to God as an act of faith, we allow Him to move in our life and work negative circumstances for our good. Our position should be: "God, I trust You. I know You're in control. Even though it didn't work out my way, You said all things work together for my good. So I believe You still have something good in my future." There is power in letting go.

Maybe you've gone through a disappointment. It wasn't fair. You don't understand it. You could easily be bitter, live with a chip on your shoulder, and give up on your dreams. No, God is at work in your life right now. He is directing your steps. What you thought was a setback is just a setup for a comeback. God is getting you in position to take you to a new level of your destiny. Now you've got to get in agreement with God. Shake off the self-pity. Shake off the disappointment. Quit thinking that God has let you down and doesn't answer your prayers. No, God has you in the palm of His hand. He is directing you every step of the way.

It may not have been fair, but God is fair. If you will let it go and move forward, God has promised to pay you back for the unfair things that have happened. As long as you're holding on to the old, it's going to keep you from the new.

There are some situations we face that there is no logical explanation for. We have to be big enough to say, "I don't understand why this happened, but I'm okay with not understanding why. I don't have to have all the answers. You are

God, and I am not. Your ways are not my ways. And since You are directing my steps, I'm not going to waste another minute trying to figure out everything that happens along the way." That's a very freeing way to live.

If you go through life trying to figure out why something bad happened, why it didn't work out, it's going to cause you to be bitter, frustrated, and confused. It will poison your life. If God wants you to know *why*, He is God and He will tell you. But if He is not revealing it to you, you need to leave it alone. Some things God doesn't want you to know. It says in Proverbs 25:2 NLT, "It is God's privilege to conceal things." If

Where you are going is much more important than where you've been. But if you stay focused on the past, you'll get stuck right where you are.

you're going to trust God, you have to accept that there are going to be unanswered questions. Everything is not going to fit perfectly into our theology, but we can come back to the central theme of who God is. God is good. God is loving. God is kind. God is fair. God is just.

In your car, there is a big windshield in the front and a very small rearview mirror. The reason is because what's in your past is not nearly as important as what's in your future. Where you are going is much more important than where you've been. But if you stay focused on the past, you'll get stuck right where you are.

If one dream has died, dream another dream. Don't let one setback define who you are. Don't let one betrayal, one mistake, one divorce, or one bankruptcy ruin the rest of your life. That is not who you are. That is just another step on the way to your divine destiny. Now let it go and step into the new beginning God has in store. Quit mourning over something you can't change. Don't put a question mark where God has put a period. If God put a period there, don't waste another minute wondering why, trying to figure it out, wallowing in self-pity and defeat. That chapter is over and done.

This is a new day. God has another opportunity in front of you. He has another relationship, another business, another breakthrough, another victory. Move forward into the new.

Action Plan

*But be doers of the word,
and not hearers only . . .*
JAMES 1:22

1. Identify anything negative from your past you may be holding on to—pain, bitterness, guilt, failures, etc.—and purposely release it to God in prayer. Let it go and determine in your heart not to think about it anymore.

2. In your heart, forgive anyone who has wronged you, not for their benefit but yours. Unforgiveness is like drinking poison and expecting the other person to die. It only hurts you. Release them and what they did to God. He is more than able to take care of it.

THINKING
YOURSELF
to
VICTORY

Fix your thoughts on what is true . . . honorable . . . right . . . pure . . . lovely . . . admirable. Think about things that are excellent and worthy of praise.

PHILIPPIANS 4:8 NLT

CHAPTER 4

Thinking Yourself to Victory

Our mind is like the control center for our life. Every decision we make and action we take begins with a thought. Our thoughts largely determine the direction of our life. If we're going to live a life of victory, we have to think the right thoughts.

Isaiah 26:3 says that if we keep our mind fixed on God, He will keep us in perfect peace. God has given us the way to have perfect peace: Keep our thoughts fixed on Him. We can't go through the day thinking, "I hope my child straightens up." "What's going to happen if I get laid off?" Or, "I might not overcome this illness." When we dwell on those kinds of thoughts, we're not going to have peace. Meditating on the problem doesn't make it better; it makes it worse.

We need to pay attention to what we're thinking about. All through the day, we should go around thinking, "God has me in the palm of His hand. All things are going to work together for my good. This problem didn't come to stay; it came to pass. Many are the afflictions of the righteous, but the Lord delivers me out of them all."

The Apostle Paul understood this principle. He said in Acts 26:2, "I think myself happy." Some people think themselves depressed. They're so focused on their problems, they think themselves discouraged. They watch so many news reports, they think themselves afraid. The good news is that just as you can think yourself depressed, fearful, or negative, you can think yourself happy. You can think yourself peaceful. You can even think yourself into a better mood.

God has given us the way to have perfect peace: Keep our thoughts fixed on Him.

Don't go through the day thinking about your problems, dwelling on who hurt you. That's going to keep you discouraged. You've got to start thinking yourself happy. All through the day, you should think, "My best days are in front of me. Something big is coming my way. What's meant for my harm, God is going to use to my advantage. My greatest victories are still in my future."

On purpose, think power thoughts. "I'm strong. I'm healthy. I'm blessed." When you wake up in the morning and those negative thoughts come—"You don't want to go to work today. You've got so many problems. You've got so much coming against you."—more than ever you need to kick it into gear. "This is going to be a great day. This is the day the Lord has made. I'm excited about my future. Something good is going to happen to me today."

Here's a key: Don't ever start the day in neutral. You can't wait to see what kind of day it's going to be; you have to *decide* what kind of day it's going to be. When you first get out of bed in the morning—before you check the news, check the weather, check to see how you feel—you need to set your mind in the right direction. "This is going to be a great day."

If you don't set your mind, the enemy will set it for you. Very often, the way we start the day will determine what kind of day we're going to have. If you start it negative, discouraged, and complaining, you are setting the tone for a lousy day. You've got to get your mind going in the right direction. Your life will follow your thoughts.

We will never rise higher than our thoughts. That's why our mind is the enemy's number one target. The enemy is called "the accuser of the brethren." He'll try to remind us of all our mistakes, failures, and shortcomings. But just like we have a remote control to change the channels on our television, we need to change the channel of our mind when those condemning, negative thoughts come. When any thought comes in our mind that is contrary to God's Word, we should immediately reject it and replace it with truth from the Word of God. God has put seeds of greatness on the inside of you. He doesn't make anything average or mediocre. But to reach your full potential, your mind has to get into agreement with what He says about you.

I'm asking you to get rid of wrong thoughts that contaminate your thinking and start meditating on what God says about you. If you'll fill your mind with the right thoughts, there won't be any room for the wrong thoughts. When you go around constantly thinking, "I'm strong. I'm healthy. I'm blessed. I've got the favor of God," then when the negative thoughts come knocking, there will be a "No Vacancy" sign. "Sorry, no room for you." They won't be able to get in.

Remember, you're going to become what you think about. Proverbs 23:7 says that as a man *thinks*, so is he. Get up every morning and set your mind in the right direction. Don't meditate on the problem; meditate on the promises of God's Word. Learn to think yourself happy. Think yourself peaceful. Think yourself victorious. Victory starts in our thinking.

If you will develop this habit of disciplining your mind to think the right thoughts and meditate on what God says, you will have more peace and more of God's favor and victory in every area of your life. And I believe and declare you will overcome every obstacle and become everything God created you to be.

Action Plan

But be doers of the word,
and not hearers only . . .
JAMES 1:22

1. Study and meditate on the scriptures in Appendix 1 on managing your thought life to get a better understanding of this principle.
2. For the next 30 days, pay special attention to your thoughts. Train yourself to quickly reject thoughts that are negative, fearful, doubtful, or otherwise contrary to the Word of God, and replace them with positive thoughts of faith, victory, and thankfulness.

The POWER *of* YOUR VISION

Where there is no vision,

the people perish . . .

PROVERBS 29:18 KJV

CHAPTER 5

The Power of Your Vision

We all have vision. Every one of us has a picture in our mind of our self, our family, our future. The question is: What does your picture look like? Do you see yourself rising higher, overcoming obstacles, and living an abundant life? Or do you have a picture of yourself struggling, defeated, addicted, overweight, and never getting good breaks? The pictures you allow in your mind will determine what kind of life you live. You have to protect your vision. If your vision is limited, your life will be limited. Proverbs 23:7 says that as a man thinks, so is he.

Before your dream can come to pass, you have to see yourself accomplishing that dream. You've got to get a picture of it. Before you lose the weight or break the addiction, you have to see it happening in your imagination. Your vision—the pictures you keep in front of you—not only drops down into your spirit but it gets into your subconscious mind. Once something is in the subconscious, it will pull you toward it like gravity without you even thinking about it.

Many people have negative images in their subconscious mind. They see themselves weak, defeated, inferior, and wonder why it feels like something is always pulling against them. It's always a struggle. They never feel good about themselves. It's because they have the wrong images.

Do you see yourself rising higher, overcoming obstacles, and living an abundant life?

If you will change those pictures and start seeing yourself the way God sees you—blessed, prosperous, healthy, strong, talented, successful—instead of having something pulling against you, it will be pulling for you. You'll be moving toward blessing, favor, promotion, and increase. Our imagination is incredibly powerful. God said of the people who were building the Tower of Babel, "Now nothing will be restrained from them, which they have imagined to do" (Genesis 11:6 KJV). Once you get a picture of something, either good or bad, you're going to move toward it.

Several years ago, a lady came down to the altar for prayer. She had just gone through a painful divorce. Her husband of many years left her for another woman. She was weeping and telling me all the reasons she would never meet anybody, how she was too old and unattractive, on and on, none of which was true. I asked her to do something to help her to get a new vision. I said, "Get a picture frame and put it on the table by your bed with no picture in it, just an empty frame. Every time you look at that frame, imagine a picture of you with the new person God is going to bring into your life."

As an act of faith, she put that picture frame there. Every time she saw it, she would begin to thank God that He was directing her steps, bringing the right person into her life, giving her beauty for her ashes. She got rid of the picture of defeat, being lonely and depressed. She started seeing herself fulfilled and full of joy with the person of her dreams.

Three years later she came back up to the altar. Once again, she was weeping, but this time they were tears of joy. She said the handsome gentleman at her side was the one she saw in her picture frame and that they were going to get married the following weekend.

What's in your picture frame? What do you see when you look into your future? More of the same? "I've reached my limits. My business will never succeed. I'll always be lonely, overweight, addicted." That's going to keep you where you are. You've got to change what's in the frame. You've got to put a new picture in there. Start seeing yourself strong, beautiful, successful, fulfilled. Your life is not going to change until you change the picture.

Proverbs 29:18 says, "Where there is no vision, the people perish." It doesn't say where there is no money, no opportunity, or no talent. What limits us is a lack of vision. Dare to dream again. Dare to have a big vision for your life, and trust God to bring it to pass. You don't have to figure out how it's going to happen. All you've got to do is believe. One touch of God's favor can bring any dream to pass. But you've got to see it on the inside before it will ever come to pass on the outside.

Dare to dream again. Dare to have a big vision for your life, and trust God to bring it to pass.

You may have been through disappointments, but this is a new day. Your greatest victories are still in your future. Get a fresh, new vision of victory for your life, and one day instead of just having a dream, you'll be living the dream. Your vision will become reality.

Action Plan

*But be doers of the word,
and not hearers only . . .*
JAMES 1:22

1. Habakkuk 2:2 says, "Write the vision and make it plain." Spend some time over the next week praying about and writing down your vision for your life. Be as specific and detailed as possible. What is your vision for your spiritual life? Relationships? Career? Finances? Health? Other areas of your life? Make sure your vision is big enough that it's going to require God's help to fulfill. It doesn't take faith if you can accomplish it on your own.

2. If you're a visual person, cut some pictures out of magazines that represent your vision for your life. Put them on your refrigerator or in your bathroom. Or use the pictures to make a "life vision" collage to provide an inspiring visual to attach your faith to.

3. If you are battling a serious illness, do like my mom when she had metastatic liver cancer and put around the house pictures of yourself when you were healthy and doing activities you enjoyed. That will help you get a vision of yourself healthy and whole again.

The POWER
of
"I AM"

From the fruit of his words a man shall be satisfied with good . . .

PROVERBS 12:14 AMP

CHAPTER 6

The Power of "I Am"

What follows the two simple words "I am" will determine what kind of life you live. "I am blessed. I am strong. I am healthy." Or, "I am slow. I am unattractive. I am a terrible mother." The "I am"s that are coming out of your mouth will bring either success or failure. All through the day the power of "I am" is at work.

We make a mistake: "I am so clumsy."

We look in the mirror: "I am so old."

We see somebody very talented: "I am so average."

We get caught in traffic: "I am so unlucky."

Many times we use the power of "I am" against us. We don't realize how it is affecting our future.

Here's the principle. What follows the "I am" will always come looking for you. That's why you have to be careful what follows the "I am." Don't ever say, "I am so unlucky. I never get any good breaks." You're inviting disappointments. "I am so broke. I am so in debt." You are inviting lack.

You need to send out some new invitations. Get up in the morning and invite good things into your life. "I am blessed. I am strong. I am talented. I am disciplined. I am focused. I am prosperous."

Our attitude should be, "I am approved by Almighty God. I am accepted. I am a masterpiece."

What kind of "I am"s are coming out of your mouth? When you have the right "I am"s, you're inviting the goodness of God.

Words have creative power. With your words you can bless or curse your future. Words are like electricity. Used the right way, it is very helpful. It gives us lights, air conditioning, all kinds of good things. But used the wrong way, electricity can be very dangerous and harm us. It's the same with our words. Proverbs 18:21 says, "Life and death are in the power of the tongue."

Don't use your words to describe your circumstances; use them to *change* your circumstances. Use your words to bless not curse your future. Joel 3:10 says, "Let the weak say, 'I am strong.'" Notice that they may be weak, but they're supposed to say, "I am strong." Not, "I am so tired. I am so rundown." That's calling in the wrong things. God tells them to declare what they want, not what their present circumstances are.

Let the poor say, "I am prosperous," not "I am broke."

Let the sick say, "I am healthy, strong, and vibrant."

If you're struggling in your finances, don't go around saying, "Business is so slow. The economy is so down. It's never going to work out."

Jesus said in Mark 11:23, "[You] will have whatever [you] say." That works in the positive or negative. By faith you've got to say, "I am blessed. I am successful. I am surrounded by God's favor."

Perhaps you've allowed what somebody said about you to hold you back—a coach, a teacher, a parent, an ex-spouse. They've planted these negative seeds of what you cannot do. "You're not smart enough. You're not talented enough. You're not disciplined enough. You're not attractive enough. You'll always make Cs. You'll always be mediocre. You'll always struggle with your weight." No, get rid of those lies. That is not who you are.

> *What follows the two simple words "I am" will determine what kind of life you live.*

You are who God says you are. Psalm 107:2 says, "Let the redeemed of the LORD say so." God wants you to "say so"—to be proactive and declare out of your mouth what His Word says about you. If you don't say so, the enemy will say so, and other people will say so.

People may have tried to push you down and tell you what you can't become. Let that go in one ear and out the other ear. What somebody said about you doesn't determine your destiny; God does. You need to know who you are and who you are not. In other words, "I am not who people say I am; I am who God says I am. I am not the tail; I am the head. I am not a borrower; I am a lender. I am not cursed; I am blessed."

Before anyone could put a curse on you, God put a blessing on you.

Before you were formed in your mother's womb, God knew you and He approved you.

When God made you, He said, "I like that. That's good. Another masterpiece!" He stamped His approval on you.

Other people may try to disapprove you, but don't go around feeling insecure or inferior. Our attitude should be, "I am approved by Almighty God. I am accepted. I am a masterpiece." When you talk like that, the seeds of greatness God has placed on the inside will begin to spring forth.

Action Plan

But be doers of the word,
and not hearers only . . .
JAMES 1:22

1. Study and meditate on the scriptures in Appendix 2 on the power of our words to get a better understanding of this spiritual principle.
2. Use the list of positive confessions in Appendix 3 to speak words of faith and victory over your life daily.

BEING SELECTIVE *about* WHAT YOU FEED YOURSELF

. . . the fool feeds on trash.

PROVERBS 15:14 NLT

CHAPTER 7

Being Selective about What You Feed Yourself

Our eyes and ears are the gateway to our soul. What we watch and listen to and who we associate with are constantly feeding us. If you eat junk food all the time—Twinkies, sodas, candy bars—you're not going to be very healthy. In the same way, if you watch things that are unwholesome, listen to things that drag you down, and associate with people who are negative and gossip, you are feeding your inner man junk food. You can't be strong in the Lord and become all God created you to be with a diet like that. You have to be extremely careful about what you take in. You are what you eat.

Today more than ever, we have the opportunity to feed on wrong things. There are over 500 channels on television. We have the Internet, smartphones, magazines, billboards. Every place we turn, there is information trying to influence us. It's not all bad, and there's nothing wrong with being entertained, but you have to stay on guard.

Proverbs 15:14 says that "the fool feeds on trash." Don't fill your mind and spirit with trash. If you put trash in, you're going to get trash out. If you watch programs where people are constantly compromising and being unfaithful in relationships, don't be surprised if you eventually find yourself doing the same. If you're watching people being dishonest, backstabbing, doing whatever they can to get ahead, that's all going into your subconscious mind. Little by little, it's desensitizing you and becoming more and more acceptable. The shock value is wearing off. Before long, you may think, "Hey, that's really no big deal. Everybody's doing it."

You're going to become what you eat. Take inventory of what you are feeding yourself. What are you watching? What are you listening to? What kind of values is it portraying? Is it wholesome, inspiring you to be better, and building you up? If not, make the necessary changes. Don't feed on trash.

Psalm 1:1 tells us not to sit inactive in the path of the ungodly. If you want to be blessed, you can't sit there passively while people gossip, tell off-color jokes, or murmur and complain. You don't have to try to straighten them out or read the Bible to them, but you should care enough about what you're feeding on to quietly step away. Don't sit inactive. When an unwholesome program or commercial comes on and you feel your internal alarm going off, don't sit inactive. Pick up the remote and change the channel. God's not going to do it for you.

You have to be proactive to guard yourself. Maybe all your friends are going to see a movie, and you don't have a good feeling about it. An alarm is going off in your spirit. Don't just go with the flow and think, "They may get upset. They may not understand. Maybe they'll think I'm old-fashioned and make fun of me." You have to ask yourself: Are you going to please people or God? Are you going to peck around with the chickens or soar like an eagle? Don't sit inactive.

Don't fill your mind and spirit with trash. If you put trash in, you're going to get trash out.

Several times in Scripture, we are compared to the eagle. Eagles are the most majestic and high soaring of all birds. That's how God sees us. He created us in His image and likeness and put seeds of greatness on the inside of us. Eagles only feed on fresh, living food, while buzzards, vultures, and crows feed on anything, including dead carcasses. The eagle derives its strength from a healthy diet. If we're going to soar like the eagle and be all God created us to be, we have to feed on good things. With modern technology, there are more ways than ever to do that. There are numerous Christian channels and other wholesome options on television. You can listen to good messages on CD in the car, on the internet, or downloaded free to your iPod. There are so many great Christian books and daily devotionals, and an abundance of good Christian music. It's easy to feed yourself the right food if you set your mind to it.

I read that the average American spends 400 hours a year in their car driving back and forth to work. Many people use that time to feed themselves the wrong things. I like to listen to the news, but I've learned the news doesn't build you up. Once you hear what you need to know, move on and use that time to feed yourself life. Listen to something that's going to help you grow and inspire you to be better.

Are you going to please people or God? Are you going to peck around with the chickens or soar like an eagle?

You are going to become what you eat. Don't feed on trash. Be an eagle. Be disciplined in what you watch and listen to. Make a decision to get rid of anything that's not building you up and helping you grow. If you will be selective in what you feed yourself, you will grow, experience more of God's favor, and I believe and declare you will become everything God created you to be.

Action Plan

But be doers of the word,
and not hearers only . . .
JAMES 1:22

1. Be quick to change the channel or station when something comes on that is not feeding your mind and spirit the right thing.

2. Don't sit inactive around coworkers and others who gossip, complain, and are negative.

3. Use your drive time and other free time to feed on anointed messages, praise music, and other material that encourages you and strengthens your faith.

DEAL *with* IT

. . . let us lay aside every weight, and the sin which so easily ensnares us . . .

Hebrews 12:1

CHAPTER 8

Deal with It

If we are going to live a victorious life in Christ, we have to be willing to deal with anything that is keeping us from being our best. It may be an addiction, a bad habit, or a hot temper. Maybe it's not getting to work on time, not treating someone right, or having a critical spirit. God is always dealing with us about something. He is always calling us higher. But anytime we go higher, our flesh has to go lower.

Sometimes we wonder why we feel stuck at the same place, why we can't seem to get out of this rut. It could be because we're not dealing with what God brings to light. When you feel that conviction on the inside—something says, "You need to treat that person better," "You need to get to work on time," "You need to get help with that bad habit"—those are not just nice thoughts. That is God speaking to you, wanting to bring you up higher. Don't ignore it. Don't sweep it under the rug.

Sometimes we think we're waiting on God when God is really waiting on us to deal with something. It may be difficult, but it's better to make right choices and be uncomfortable for a while than to keep going the same way and miss your destiny.

But many people choose what is comfortable now and then wonder why they don't have victory. It was an eleven-day journey to the Promised Land, but the people of Israel went around the same mountain for forty years and never made it in. They were complainers, negative, ungrateful. God gave them chance after chance, but they kept failing the test. They didn't deal with it and missed out on God's best.

If you have an area you struggle in—and we all do—don't ignore it, pretend it's not there, or hope it just goes away. You will never conquer what you don't confront.

If you have an area you struggle in—and we all do—don't ignore it. Don't pretend it's not there or hope it just goes away. You will never conquer what you don't confront. If you have a problem, get it out in the open. "God, every time I see my friend, she's so talented, she's so beautiful, I tend to get jealous. God, help me." Or, "God, these people really hurt me. I'm having a problem forgiving them. God, I've got this resentment in my heart." When you have a humble attitude, asking God for help in faith, He will never let you down. If you do your part and deal with it, God will do His part and help you overcome.

When God asks us to do something difficult—forgive someone who hurt us, walk away from a friend who is polluting our life, or anything that's a major sacrifice or takes great effort—we can be assured a major blessing will follow our obedience. There is a blessing attached to every act of obedience. If we cooperate with God, there will be a major shift in our life for the better.

I say every day, "God, search my heart. Am I on the right track? God, show me areas I need to improve in. What can I do better?" God doesn't require us to be perfect. All He asks is that we keep trying and taking steps to improve. We should treat people better this year than we did last year. We should have more discipline, less bad habits, a better attitude. If you're stuck at the same place, you need to pray, "God, show me what I need to do to improve."

You and God are a majority.

There will always be something that stands between you and your destiny: pride, jealousy, an offense, a bad habit. The enemy will give you the low ground. He doesn't mind you being average or mediocre, not making a difference. But when you determine not to live with things holding you back, deal with issues God brings to your attention, and decide to be all He created you to be, you're going to see God's favor in amazing ways.

I'm asking you to shake off any kind of mediocrity. You have seeds of greatness on the inside. There's no obstacle too big, no addiction too great, no bad habit too strong. You and God are a majority. As you deal with what He brings to light and do your best to walk in obedience, you'll experience God's radical favor, blessings, and miraculous turnarounds.

Action Plan

*But be doers of the word,
and not hearers only . . .*
JAMES 1:22

1. Spend some time alone with God and pray as David did in Psalm 139:23–24: "Search me, O God, and know my heart... Point out anything in me that offends you, and lead me along the path of everlasting life." Be willing to openly and honestly confront anything He brings to your attention.

2. Be willing to get outside help to overcome any addiction, bad habit, or other issue that is holding you back. Seek counseling, attend some classes, or participate in a recovery program. Be determined to do everything you can in the natural, and God will do what you can't do in the supernatural.

3. Seek out a prayer/accountability partner who can offer prayer, support, and encouragement when you are dealing with a difficult issue. James 5:16 says, "Confess your sins to each other [not just to God] and pray for each other so that you may be healed." When we bring an issue into the light and confess it to a trusted person, it immediately has less power over us.

Scriptures on Managing Our Thought Life

1. "For as he thinks in his heart, so is he."—Proverbs 23:7

COMMENT: This verse tells us that *we become what we think about.* Our life will follow our most dominant thoughts. It's like the saying: "Whether you think you can or think you can't, you're right." Ten out of the twelve spies Moses sent to spy out the Promised Land came back saying, "There are giants in the land, and we are like grasshoppers compared to them" (Numbers 13:33, paraphrased). They didn't see themselves as able, and none of them entered into the Promised Land. But two spies, Joshua and Caleb, said, "Let us go up at once and take possession, for we are well able to overcome it" (Numbers 13:30). They were the only two people from that generation of Israelites to enter the Promised Land.

Do you see yourself as well able to do what God has called you to do, or do you see yourself as a grasshopper?

2. "Finally, brethren, whatever is true, whatever is honorable, whatever is right, whatever is pure, whatever is lovely, whatever is of good repute, if there is *any* excellence and if *anything* worthy of praise, *dwell* on these things."—Philippians 4:8 NASB, emphasis added

    COMMENT: This verse tells us to dwell on what is good in our life, not what's wrong. Dwell on God and His truth, not our problems. Dwell on positive, faith-filled thoughts. We are the only ones who can manage our thought life; God is not going to do it for us. We have to choose to dwell on thoughts that are going to lead to victory, not defeat.

3. "And do not be conformed to this world, but be transformed by the renewing of your mind . . ."—Romans 12:2

    COMMENT: This verse tells us not to think and act like the world, and it tells us how to be transformed— by renewing our mind. How do we renew our mind? By filling it daily with the Word of God, praise music, anointed messages, and positive confessions.

4. "And be constantly renewed in the spirit of your mind [having a fresh mental and spiritual attitude]."—Ephesians 4:23 AMP

   COMMENT: This verse tells us that renewing our mind is not a once-in-the-morning thing, but something we have to do "constantly" all throughout the day.

5. ". . . we take captive every thought to make it obedient to Christ."—2 Corinthians 10:5 NIV

   COMMENT: Like the previous verse that talked about "constantly" renewing our mind, this verse tells us to take every single thought "captive" to make it obedient to Christ. God is telling us to manage our thought life so that every thought lines up with His Word. When a thought comes in that doesn't line up with His Word, we need to be proactive to reject it and replace it with thoughts that do.

6. "You will keep him in perfect peace, whose mind is stayed on You."—Isaiah 26:3

   COMMENT: This verse tells us how to stay in perfect peace, no matter what's going on in our life: Keep our mind *stayed* on God. Not our problems, what's going on in the economy and world, or what people are saying and doing, but keep our mind stayed on God. If we'll do that, He promises to keep us in not just peace, but *perfect* peace.

7. "Set your mind on things above, not on things on the earth."—Colossians 3:2

COMMENT: Like the previous verse that tells us to keep our mind stayed on God, this one tells us to *set* our mind on things above, not what's going on in this earthly plane. The key word is *set*. We have to set our minds on things above; God is not going to set it for us. And if we don't set it, the enemy will set it, our emotions will set it, our circumstances will set it, and people will set it. We have to actively set our mind on the right things all day long.

APPENDIX 2

Scriptures on the Power of Our Words

1. "Death and life are in the power of the tongue . . ."
   —Proverbs 18:21

   COMMENT: By our own tongue, the Bible says we have the power to speak death or life over ourselves and our circumstances, our children, finances, or a loved one who is sick. Notice how the emphasis in this verse is not on the power of death and life, but the power of the *tongue.*

2. "Words are powerful; take them seriously. Words can be your salvation. Words can be your damnation."
   —Matthew 12:36–37 MSG

COMMENT: Jesus corroborates the previous verse, telling us that our words have the power to "make us or break us."

3. "For assuredly, I say to you, whoever says to this mountain, 'Be removed and be cast into the sea,' and does not doubt in his heart, but believes that those things he says will come to pass, he will have whatever he says."—Mark 11:23

COMMENT: Jesus didn't tell us here to just pray about the mountain, but *speak to* the mountain. This applies to any "mountain" in our life, whether it's an illness, financial problem, etc. He goes on to say that if we don't doubt in our heart, we will have *whatever* things we say. If we speak negatively, we'll get negative results; if we speak positively, we'll get positive results.

4. "Indeed, we put bits in horses' mouths that they may obey us, and we turn their whole body. Look also at ships: although they are so large and are driven by fierce winds, they are turned by a very small rudder wherever the pilot desires. Even so the tongue is a little member and boasts great things."—James 3:3–5

COMMENT: This verse makes it so clear that our tongue determines the whole direction of our life—just like the bit in a horse's mouth or the rudder of a ship determines its direction.

5. "... he who has My word, let him speak My word faithfully.... 'Is not My word like a fire?' says the LORD, 'and like a hammer that breaks the rock in pieces?'"—Jeremiah 23:28–29

6. "A man will be satisfied with good by the fruit of his mouth..."—Proverbs 12:14

COMMENT: This amazing verse tells us so clearly how to be satisfied with good: by the fruit (words) of our mouth. If we want to be satisfied with good, we have to speak words of faith and victory out of our mouth at all times.

7. "And they [the saints] overcame him [the devil, the accuser of the brethren] by the blood of the Lamb and by the word of their testimony..."—Revelation 12:11

COMMENT: This verse doesn't say we overcome the devil with the *thought* of our testimony, but the *word* of our testimony. Our "testimony" is what God's Word says about us. Everything else is either a lie from the enemy or wrong thinking on our part. The word of your testimony has to be spoken, like Jesus did when He was tempted by the devil in the wilderness. He told the devil three times, "It is written . . ." in Matthew 4:4–10. He quoted Scripture to him and declared what the Word of God said about Him, and the devil eventually left Him (Matthew 4:11).

8. "He who guards his mouth keeps his life, but he who opens wide his lips shall have destruction."—Proverbs 13:3

9. "Whoever guards his mouth and tongue keeps his soul from troubles."—Proverbs 21:23

10. "You are snared by the words of your mouth . . ." —Proverbs 6:2

Daily Positive Confessions

"[You] will have whatever [you] say."
MARK 11:23

Many times, the way we start the day determines what kind of day we're going to have. That's why it's so important that we get our mind going in the right direction first thing in the morning. And that's why the enemy loves to attack our mind the minute we wake up. Use these positive confessions to speak out loud every morning to get your mind and mouth in agreement with God and programmed for victory. Memorize as many as you can, and meditate on them and speak them over yourself throughout the day. The thoughts you think and words you speak today will determine your tomorrow.

- I am blessed.
- I am forgiven and redeemed.

- I am loved, accepted, and approved.

- I am free—free from sickness, poverty, lack, and every kind of bondage or stronghold.

- I am secure and confident.

- I am wise, intelligent, and creative.

- I am focused and disciplined.

- I am successful.

- I am talented.

- I am anointed.

- I am prosperous.

- I am healthy.

- I am full of vim, vigor, vitality, energy, and strength.

- I am God's masterpiece, created in His image and likeness.

- I am a person of divine purpose and destiny.

- I am a child of the Most High God.

- In all things I am more than a conqueror (Romans 8:37).

- I can do all things through Christ who strengthens me (Philippians 4:13).

- God always causes me to triumph in Christ Jesus (2 Corinthians 2:14).

- God has plans to prosper me, to give me a hope and a future (Jeremiah 29:11).

- God's favor surrounds me like a shield (Psalm 5:12).

- God's goodness and mercy follow me all the days of my life (Psalm 23:6).

- My path is like the shining sun, shining brighter and brighter until the full day (Proverbs 4:18).

- God is perfecting everything that concerns me (Psalm 138:8).

Prayer of Salvation

If you have never formally asked Jesus to be your Lord and Savior, or maybe you've grown cold toward the Lord and need to rededicate your life, I invite you to take a minute and do that now. The Bible says *today* is the day of salvation because tomorrow is not guaranteed. You may not have the opportunity to make this decision later, so don't put it off. Pray this simple prayer and ask Jesus into your heart:

> *Lord Jesus, I repent of all my sins. I ask You to come into my heart and wash me clean. I make you my Lord and Savior. Thank you, Jesus, for saving me and making me a part of the family of God. Help me to follow You all of my days. In Jesus' name, Amen.*

If you prayed that simple prayer, the Bible says you were "born again." That just means you have a brand new life in Christ. You are no longer separated from God in sin. Jesus paid the price for all your sins—past, present, and future—so you could be in the family of God. The Bible also says you are a new creation in Christ. You may not feel any different at first, but as you continue walking with Christ, you will gradually become more like Him.

Next Steps

To help you grow in your walk with the Lord,
I encourage you to:

1. Get into a good Bible-teaching church.
2. Don't spend time with friends who are going to pull you away from your walk with the Lord. Instead, invite them to come to church with you.
3. Talk to God daily through prayer. You don't need to pray fancy prayers, just be yourself and talk to God like a loving Father.
4. Read your Bible daily to gain a deeper understanding of God and the Christian life.
5. As a person who represents Jesus on the earth, demonstrate love and concern for others.
6. Tell others about Jesus.

STAY**CONNECTED,**
BE**BLESSED.**

From thoughtful articles to powerful blogs,
podcasts and more, JoelOsteen.com is full of
inspirations that will give you encouragement and
confidence in your daily life.

AVAILABLE ON JOELOSTEEN.COM

today's WORD

This daily devotional from Joel
and Victoria will help you grow
in your relationship with the Lord
and equip you to be everything
God intends you to be.

Joel Osteen
STREAMING

Miss a broadcast? Watch Joel
Osteen on demand, and see
Joel LIVE on Sundays.

Joel Osteen
PODCAST

The podcast is a great way
to listen to Joel where you
want, when you want.

CONNECT WITH US

PUT JOEL IN YOUR POCKET

Join our
community of
believers on your
favorite social
network.

Get the inspiration and
encouragement of Joel Osteen
on your iPhone, iPad or Android
device! Our app puts Joel's
messages, devotions and more
at your fingertips.

Thanks for helping us make a difference in
the lives of millions around the world.